Little Rose of Sharon

Nan Gurley

Illustrated by Tim Jonke

Chariot Victor Publishing
A Division of Cook Communications

Chariot Victor Publishing,
A division of Cook Communications, Colorado Springs, Colorado 80918
Cook Communications, Paris, Ontario
Kingsway Communications, Eastbourne, England

LITTLE ROSE OF SHARON
© 1998 by Nan Gurley for text, illustrations by Tim Jonke.
Printed in Canada.

Editor: Liz Duckworth
Designer: Andrea Boven

    4 5 6 7 8 9 10 Printing/Year 02 01 00 99 98

Library of Congress Cataloging-in-Publication Data

Gurley, Nan
        Little rose of Sharon/Nan Gurley
            p. cm.
        Summary: When the little rose of Sharon sacrifices her beautiful red petals
to save a baby dove, she hears the Creator say that her love is like that of His Son.
        ISBN 0-7814-3031-3
        [1. Rose of Sharon—Fiction. 2. Love—Fiction. 3. Generosity—Fiction.
4. Jesus Christ—Love.] I. Title.
PZ7.G981485 Li 1998
[E]—dc21
                                                                    98-12753
                                                                    CIP
                                                                    AC

For Wayne, who always believed
N.G.

For Virginia and Albert Jonke
T.J.

Spring came to the newly made world, and every day a certain little rose grew taller and more beautiful. "Surely the Creator will be proud of me," she hoped, as the color deepened in her petals.

The little rose watched as the hills and Valley of Sharon came to life. Daffodils grew on the hillside. Almond trees bloomed full and white. And the sweet smell of myrtle blossoms filled the air.

As the large green leaves on the fig tree above her danced gently in the breeze, the little rose looked up and saw a dove sitting on a nest made of twigs and grass. Inside the nest was a tiny white egg.

While the mother dove flew over the hillside looking for seeds and nuts, the father dove sat on the egg and made soft cooing sounds. "Some day very soon," thought the little rose, "the baby dove will hatch out of its egg."

arly one morning as the
sun peeked over the eastern
sky, the little rose saw the
Creator. He was walking
through the cool grass,
looking at all His trees and
flowers. Sometimes He would
stop for a moment and listen
to a bird's song, or sit in the
shade of an olive tree and
watch the sheep grazing on
distant hills.

The little rose stood straight
and tall and opened her petals
as far as she could. She hoped
the Creator would notice her
as He walked by.

Soon He came walking toward her. "Surely the Creator will be pleased with my beautiful petals," she thought happily. Then the Creator stood before her. For a long time, He looked down at her deep red petals and smiled. Before He turned to go, He bent down and breathed her sweet smell.

The little rose felt her heart would burst with joy. "He noticed me," she thought, "and He smiled at me! Truly, He must think I am beautiful."

Later that evening, as she drifted off to sleep, the little rose was still remembering the smile of the Creator.

During the night, a storm rolled in from the Mediterranean Sea. The wind howled through the trees, and the rain beat down on the shrubs and flowers.

The little rose bent and swayed in the storm. She was frightened of losing her petals. As the rain beat against her, she held on to her petals with all her strength.

Finally, the storm ended. When morning light filled the sky, the little rose was proud to see that none of her petals had fallen to the ground.

But when she looked down, she saw a white shape on the ground below her. It was the tiny dove's egg, nestled deeply in the grass.

"It must have fallen out of the nest during the storm," she thought. "Surely the mother and father dove will find it." She wished she could call out to them and tell them where the egg was lying, but she could only watch as the doves flew back and forth looking for the egg and making sad and mournful sounds.

All day the doves searched for the tiny egg, but they never saw it in the grass beneath the rose. When the sky began to darken, the doves flew back to the branches of the fig tree.

"If the egg is not kept warm, the baby dove inside it will die," thought the little rose as the cool evening breeze began to blow.

She was sad to think that the baby dove might never break out of its shell and learn to fly. "If only I could keep it warm."

As the moon slowly rose in the sky, covering the earth with a silver light, the little rose thought of the only way she could keep the egg warm through the chilly night. One by one, she dropped her petals and covered the tiny white dove's egg. When the last one fell and the rose petal blanket was complete, the little rose fell asleep to the mournful cooing of the doves.

Early the next morning, the little rose was wakened by tiny chirping sounds. "What could it be?" she wondered. And then she noticed the smallest movement beneath the fallen petals.

Suddenly, a tiny dove's beak poked out from beneath the rose petal blanket. "The baby dove is alive!" she thought with joy as the chirping grew louder.

The mother and father heard the baby dove and flew down from the fig tree. The little rose watched as they lifted their baby from the rose petals and carried it back to their nest.

$\mathcal{L}$ater that morning as the little rose was listening to the gentle cooing of the doves, she saw the Creator walking on the hillside. "Oh dear," she thought, "I hope He doesn't notice me. Without my petals I am no longer beautiful." The little rose was so ashamed, she looked down. But when the Creator stood before her, He gently reached out and touched her stem.

"You have given all you had to save the life of the baby dove," said the Creator. The little rose felt warm inside at the sound of His voice. "One day when My Son lives on this earth, He too will give everything He has." The little rose looked up into the gentle eyes of the Creator. "Because of the love you have shown for the baby dove, I will call My Son the Rose of Sharon, for He too will give everything He has and show the world My love."

The Creator tenderly touched her stem once more and as He walked on through the hillside, the little rose joyfully lifted her face to the warm light of the sun.